WELCOME TO MY COUNTRY

IRAQ

Written by: Sonali Malhotra
Editors: Cheryl Sim and Melvin Neo
Designer: Benson Tan
Photo research: Thomas Khoo

PICTURE CREDITS

Agence France Presse: 3 (bottom), 22, 38 (bottom)
Art Directors & TRIP Photo Library: 5, 7, 15 (top), 17, 18 (bottom), 24, 29, 33, 44 (both)
Tor Eigeland: 37
Getty Images/Hulton Archive: 15 (bottom), 38 (top)
Haga Library, Japan: 4, 6, 32, 34
HBL Photo Network Agency: 3 (top),14, 16 (top), 23
Hutchison Library: cover, 1, 20
Klingwalls Geografiska Fárgfotos: 8, 12, 13, 16 (bottom), 30, 31, 41
North Wind Picture Archive: 2, 11
Christine Osborne Pictures: 18 (top), 19
Jaime Simson: 3 (centre), 21, 26
Nik Wheeler: 9, 10, 25, 27, 28, 35, 36, 39, 40, 43, 45

This edition published in 2010
by Franklin Watts

Designed and originated by
Marshall Cavendish International (Asia) Pte Ltd

Franklin Watts
338 Euston Road
London NW1 3BH

Dewey number 956.7'0443

ISBN 978 1 4451 0203 0

Franklin Watts is a division of Hachette Children's Books,
an Hachette UK company.
www.hachette.co.uk

Printed in Malaysia

Contents

Words that appear in the glossary are printed in **boldface** type the first time they occur in the text.

Babylon is an ancient city in Iraq. Many of the groups that ruled the region used Babylon as their capital city.

Welcome to Iraq!

The Republic of Iraq has a very rich and colourful history dating back thousands of years. Located in the Middle East, the country has ancient rivers, vast deserts and rugged mountains. Iraq became independent in 1932. From 1968 to 2003, Iraq was under the rule of a **dictator**. Let's learn more about this ancient land and its people.

This Kurdish man is selling vegetables at a stand. The Kurds are an **ethnic** group that lives in northern Iraq.

The Flag of Iraq

The flag of Iraq has three horizontal stripes –red, white and black. The new flag was approved by the Iraqi parliament in 2008. Written in the white stripe in green script are the words '*Allahu Akbar*' (ah-LAH-who AHK-bar), which means 'God is great'.

The Land

Iraq occupies a land area of 438,317 square kilometres. Its neighbours are Saudi Arabia, Turkey, Iran, Kuwait, Jordan and Syria. In the southeast, Iraq has a coastline of 58 kilometres that borders the Persian Gulf. Iraq's two main rivers are the Euphrates and the Tigris. The rivers offer Iraqis water for crops, for drinking and for travel.

Baghdad, Iraq's capital and its largest city, is located on the banks of the Tigris River. The city's location has played an important role in the history of Iraq.

Iraq has mountains in the north and deserts in the south. In between are lush, green valleys.

Rugged mountains cover much of Iraq's northern and eastern areas. Towering 3,611 metres above ground, the country's highest peak is located in the vast Zagros mountain range which borders Iraq and Iran. Though previously unnamed, the local Kurdish people refer to this point as Cheekha Dar, which means 'black tent'. To the west of the mountains, the land is good for farming. Large plains cover a vast portion of central Iraq. The south and southwest of the country are covered in desert regions. The dry land is so harsh that few people live there.

Climate

Iraq has a dry season and a wet season. The country's dry season is from May to October. Iraq's wet season is from November to April. During the wet season, the country can get almost 102 centimetres of rain.

In summer, temperatures can reach up to 51° Celsius. Winter temperatures in Iraq are mild and do not often go below freezing, except in the northern mountains.

These people are harvesting parsley on the outskirts of Baghdad. Summers are very hot and winters are mild.

Camels can live without food and water for many days, which makes them useful for travelling across the deserts of Iraq. Camels are known as the 'ships of the desert' because of the way they seem to float across the sand while walking.

Plants and Animals

Many kinds of plant grow in Iraq, from junipers and wild pears in the mountains to willows and **liquorice** along the Tigris and Euphrates rivers. Plantain grows in the plains and date palms grow all over the country.

A variety of animals can be found in Iraq, including mountain goats, deer, wild pigs, foxes and wildcats. Partridges, vultures and hawks are just a few of the birds that live in the country.

History

Between 3500 and 2400 BCE, the Sumerians lived in what is now Iraq. At that time, the country was called Mesopotamia, or 'the land between two rivers', because it was located between the Tigris and Euphrates rivers. The Sumerians invented the wheel, the calendar, the plough and writing. In 2340 BCE, the Sumerians lost their **empire** to the Akkadians, who then ruled for two hundred years.

The Sumerians knew a lot about building strong structures and temples. Many of the buildings that the Sumerians created, such as this one in the ancient city of Babylon, are still standing today.

The Code of Hammurabi gave Babylonians a strict set of rules about marriage, business, property and slavery. The code was carved into a tall, black stone pillar called a stele, which was placed in public for all to see and obey.

After the Akkadians lost power, many different groups ruled the country. In 1792 BCE, King Hammurabi took over. He named his new empire Babylonia and made Babylon the capital city. The empire began to weaken after the king's death and was split into two parts–Babylon and Assyria. By 539 BCE, Babylon had been taken over by invaders from what is now Iran. In 320 BCE, Alexander the Great **conquered** Babylon and Assyria.

The Abbasids valued the arts and learning. During their rule, they built beautiful buildings like the Al-Askari **Mosque** in Samarra. The rule of the Abbasids is called the golden age of culture and the arts in Iraq.

Invasions and Empires

In the eighth century CE, a group of Arabs called the Abbasids invaded Iraq. Baghdad became their capital city. Many people came to Baghdad to study medicine, mathematics and the arts. In 1258, the Mongols from central Asia conquered Iraq. Later, the Ottoman Turks began to take over the country. In 1534, they took control of Baghdad. The Ottoman Empire ruled Iraq until 1917.

Modern Times

From 1920 to 1932, Britain ruled Iraq. After Iraq gained its independence, it became a **monarchy**. In 1958, an Iraqi military group killed the prime minister and king. The group then took over and made Iraq a **republic**. Other groups later fought for control until, in 1979, Saddam Hussein became president. He ruled as a dictator until 2003.

The Freedom Monument is located in Al-Tahrir Square in Baghdad. It was built in honour of the 1958 **uprising** in Iraq.

Iraq at War

In 1980, under Saddam Hussein, Iraq invaded Iran. The war ended in 1988 with no clear winner. In 1990, Iraq invaded Kuwait. A group of nations, led by the United States, forced the Iraqis out of Kuwait in the Persian Gulf War. In 2003, the U.S. and Britain went to war with Iraq again and removed Saddam Hussein from power. They believed Iraq was making weapons that could kill millions of people. Since then, Iraq has been moving towards restoring peace and stability in the country.

After the Persian Gulf War (1990–1991), the United Nations (UN) made rules about the weapons Iraq could have. Experts, such as these inspectors, were sent to watch over the country's weapons factories. For over ten years, however, Saddam Hussein would not let them into some places, which led to the 2003 invasion of Iraq by the United States and Britain.

Nebuchadnezzar II (c.630 BCE–562 BCE)

Nebuchadnezzar ruled Babylon, one of the two kingdoms formed when the old Babylonian empire fell apart. The king was very interested in architecture and had many great structures built, such as the Ishtar Gate and the famous Hanging Gardens of Babylon.

King Faisal I (1885–1933)

In 1921, the British selected Faisal I to become king of Iraq. A vote by the Iraqi people made it official. During his rule, Faisal helped the country become independent. He also helped Iraq join the League of Nations.

King Faisal I

Nuri es-Said (1888–1958)

Nuri es-Said

As prime minister from 1953 to 1958, Nuri es-Said helped Iraq become more modern and to trade with other nations. He was killed in 1958 when a military group took over the country.

The Government and the Economy

From 1968 to 2003, the Ba'ath Party was the only political organization in Iraq. It was led by Saddam Hussein, who later served as president and prime minister of the country.

Iraq's Council of Representatives has 275 members who serve a four-year term each. Iraq has eighteen **provinces** which are run by their own elected provincial government.

In 1979, when he first came to power, Saddam Hussein had the support of nations around the world. Because of crimes against his own people, especially the Kurds, he is now believed to have been one of the most violent and dangerous dictators in history. He was executed in 2006 for his war crimes.

Before the war in 2003, paintings and statues of Saddam Hussein could be found on display all over Iraq. Most are now gone.

For most of modern Iraq's history, Kurds and other minority groups were not treated as equals to the majority Arab population. Under Saddam Hussein's rule, Kurds were not allowed to serve in the government. Today, Kurds and other minorities are able to participate in politics without **oppression**. As a Kurd, Jalal Talabani has made history as Iraq's first non-Arab president.

The Court System

Iraq's court system has three levels. The country's highest court is the Federal Supreme Court. Iraq's religious courts hear cases about religion, marriage and **inheritance**. Special courts hear cases about national security.

The Presidency

Jalal Talabani has been in office since 2005. He is also the first president to be elected under Iraq's new **constitution**, which came into force that same year. A president is allowed to serve for two terms, each lasting four years.

Economy

Years of war have weakened Iraq's economy. The country is a producer of natural gas, salt, sulphur and **phosphates**. Electricity, fuel, textiles, building materials and chemicals are also made to be sold to other countries. Although it is estimated that 75 per cent of the population work in agriculture, only 5 per cent of food and livestock is produced for **export**, with most farming produce used for local consumption.

The money earned from these resources and other industries alone is not enough to drive Iraq's economy. Fortunately, Iraq has the world's third largest oil reserves.

These oil pipelines run through Iraq's Kurdish region. Many pipelines were left unused after Iraq was restricted from selling more of its oil. Today, these pipelines have been reopened or upgraded, and new ones also built, so that Iraq can export more oil to recover from years of war and poverty.

Iraq has many date plantations. Not much of the harvests can be exported due to poor quality, and thousands of tons are wasted every year. In 2009, the government approved a plan to turn large amounts of the unused fruit into biofuel. If successful, this alternative source of energy will be sold to other countries for profit.

After the 1990 Persian Gulf War, Iraq could only sell a limited amount of oil to other nations. The rules were made so that Iraq would be unable to afford to build dangerous and expensive weapons. Between 1995 and 2003, the UN allowed Iraq to export oil in return for medicines and food. With these restrictions now lifted, Iraq is once again depending heavily on oil, its most valuable resource, to mend its economy.

Tank trucks transport oil across Iraq. During the Persian Gulf War, many of Iraq's oil plants were destroyed.

People and Lifestyle

Most Iraqis are Arabs who belong to the religion of Islam. Some Christians and Jews also live in Iraq. Many Iraqis have moved to the cities, where they hope to find better-paying jobs.

Ethnic Groups

After Arabs, Kurds are Iraq's second largest ethnic group. They live in the mountainous areas of northeastern Iraq.

The Kurds lead simple lives. Most Kurds work as shepherds or farmers. In recent times, however, many Kurds have moved to cities in search of jobs.

The Ma'dan, who live in the marshes of southern Iraq, build their houses out of reeds. The homes have no running water or electricity and are built above the ground to stay dry.

The Ma'dan (MAH-dan), or Marsh Arabs, live in the marshlands between the Euphrates and Tigris rivers. The Ma'dan are good at fishing and hunting for their own food.

The Bedouin are **nomads** and often live in tents made of woven goat or camel hair. They follow their herds of sheep and goats as they roam through the desert.

Other ethnic groups in Iraq include the Turkomans, the Yazidis (yah-ZEE-deez) and the Sabeans.

Family Life

Iraqi families are usually large and family relationships are close. Most families live in one house, which is expanded when the family grows. It is common for children to live with their parents until they reach their mid-twenties.

Most Iraqi marriages are arranged by the couple's parents. The groom signs a contract to make the marriage official.

A group of Yazidi men and women has gathered in Mosul to pray. Yazidis are a very close-knit people. They hardly ever mix with other ethnic groups, and the men and women rarely marry anyone who is not from the community.

Unlike some other Islamic countries in the Middle East, the women in Iraq are not required to wear an *abbayah* (ah-BYE-ah), a long gown with a veil that covers most of a woman's face. Muslim women in Iraq often do wear a *hijab* (hih-JOB), which is a head scarf that does not cover their faces.

Women in Iraq

In the past, Iraqi women settled down young to raise a family. In the 1920s, many women began to enter the **workforce**. After the Persian Gulf War (1990–1991), the bad economy forced many people to lose their jobs. Women suffered further under the Hussein government, which created laws against them working. Women have since been allowed to enter politics. Women now make up a large part of the Iraqi government and help speak up for women's rights, such as voting and equal education opportunities.

Education

In Iraq, education is considered to be very important. In 1850, only 1 per cent of all Iraqis was able to read and write. Today, the literacy rate has risen to more than 70 per cent. Schooling is free for Iraqi children and they must attend classes from age six to age eleven.

Iraq is one of the few Arab countries that encourages girls to receive an education. In addition, both men and women can serve as teachers.

All children in Iraq, including these students in Baghdad, must attend classes. Even the smallest Iraqi villages have their own schools.

In Iraq, children often take classes outside of school, such as this art class being held in Baghdad.

About half of all Iraqi students go on to secondary school, which lasts six years. In their third year, students can choose to take **vocational** classes.

Iraq has eight universities. Four are located in Baghdad. The others are in Arbil, Mosul, Al Basrah and Tikrit. Iraq also has institutions that teach subjects such as farming and **technology**.

Religion

About 97 per cent of Iraq's population are Muslims, or followers of Islam. They must live by a set of religious rules called the Five Pillars of Islam. The rules include reciting, 'There is no God but Allah, and Muhammad is His messenger', praying five times a day, giving money to the poor, fasting during the Islamic holy month and making at least one **pilgrimage** to the holy city of Mecca, in Saudi Arabia.

This gold-domed mosque, called the Mosque of Imam Ali, is one example of Islamic architecture. Since the Islamic religion came to Iraq in the seventh century, Muslims have been building majestic mosques all across the country.

In Iraq, Christians go to churches, such as the Church of Tahira in the city of Qaraqosh, to pray. The country forbids Christians to talk about their faith or hold any religious event outside of their church.

Muslims in Iraq are divided into two groups: the Shi'ites and the Sunnis. The Shi'ites believe that only relatives of the prophet Muhammad can serve as religious leaders. The Sunnis believe that anyone educated in the Islamic religion can lead.

Of the small number of Iraqis who are non-Muslim, Christians make up the largest group. Most Christian Iraqis are Roman Catholic.

Language

Iraq's official language is Arabic, which is read from right to left. The language's twenty-eight letters are written differently depending on where they fall: at the beginning, middle or end of a word. Arabic is a difficult language to speak because many of the sounds are made deep in the throat and are hard to learn.

Because most Iraqis can read, bookstalls such as this one in Baghdad are very popular.

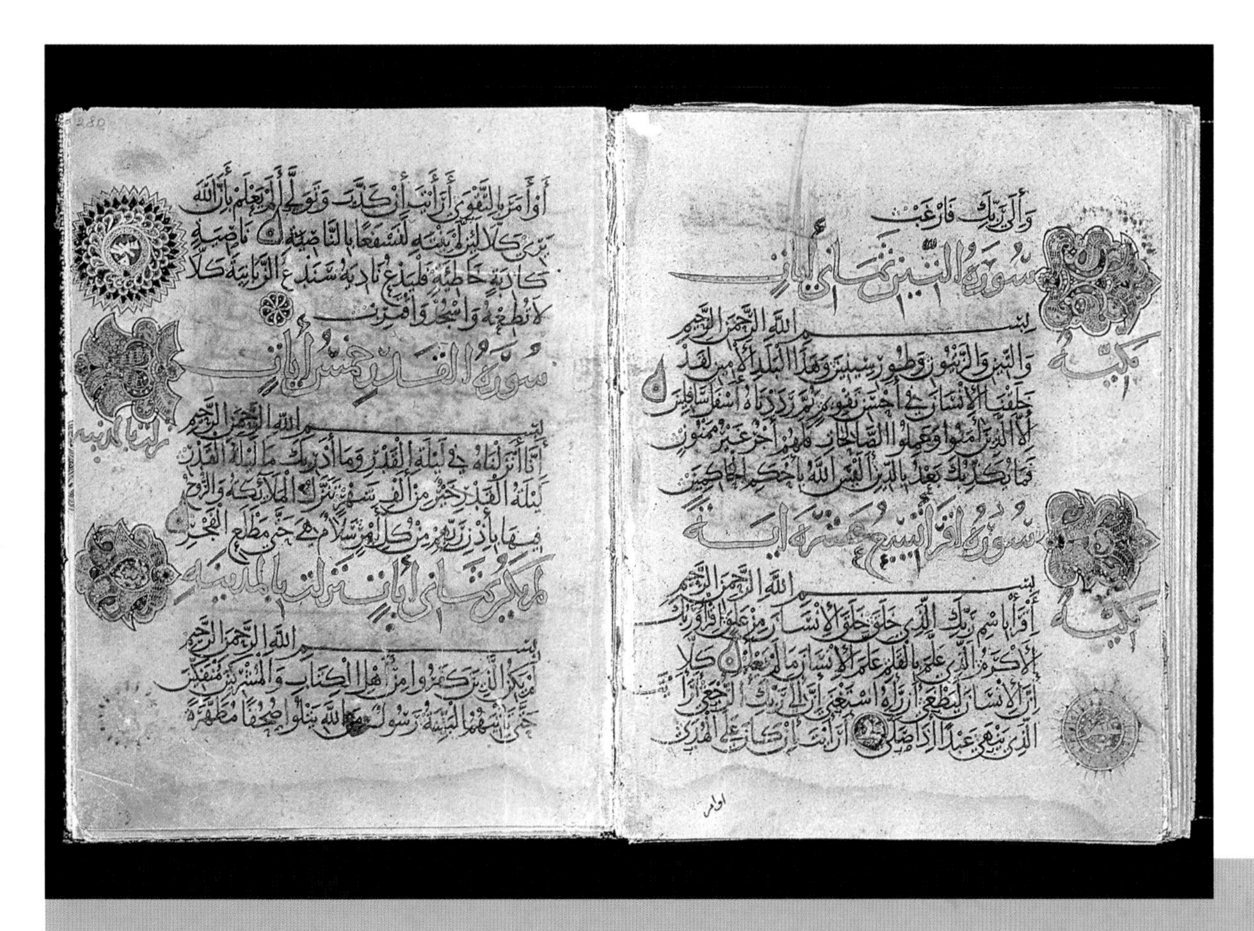

Antique copies of the Koran, the Islamic holy book, are found in many of Iraq's museums. The books were handwritten in Arabic, which is made up of characters with graceful loops and swirls.

Literature

Because some of the world's earliest examples of writing have been found in Iraq, experts believe written language may have started in that land.

Iraq has produced many authors and poets, including Muhammad Mahdi al-Jawahiri (1900–1997) and Nazik al-Malaika (1922–2007).

Arts

Iraq has a rich tradition in architecture, pottery, painting, music and weaving. Iraqi art is largely influenced by Islam, which does not allow artists to show images of people. Most artwork in Iraq is done in **arabesque**, which uses lots of flower shapes, circles, squares and other patterns.

The people of Iraq value art. Often, the country's museums pay local artists to create artworks they can exhibit.

This young Iraqi painter is pictured at work in his studio. Many Iraqis enjoy the arts, including music, painting and sculpture.

Architecture in Baghdad is a mix of the old and the new. Ancient monuments stand next to new, modern buildings, which creates an interesting blend of styles.

In Iraq, writing the Arabic language in **calligraphy** is a popular art form. It is often used to decorate buildings and mosques but may also decorate tiles, plates or sculptures. Most messages in calligraphy come from the Koran.

Many of the country's monuments and buildings have artistic styles, too. During the rule of Saddam Hussein, architects were ordered only to create buildings in acceptable Iraqi styles.

Dance

Folk dancing is a popular form of entertainment in Iraq. Each region of the country has its own folk dances. During the Kurdish New Year which falls on March 21, and at weddings, the Kurds perform a dance within a larger circle of dancers. The Bedouin have their own dance, the Hagallah, which is danced in a line. The Hagallah is performed during the date harvest.

Many folk dances in Iraq are designed to help men and women meet and find future wives and husbands. To draw attention, the dancers often wear colourful costumes.

The oud, rebaba and riqq, along with various hand drums, are instruments used to play traditional Iraqi music.

Music

Traditional Iraqi music is very lively. The performers often **chant**, clap their hands or play drums. Iraq has several traditional instruments, including the *oud* (OOD), which is shaped like a guitar. The *riqq* (REEK), a kind of tambourine, usually keeps the beat alongside other traditional instruments. Bedouin musicians often play the *rebaba* (rah-BAH-bah), a one-stringed, fiddle-like instrument.

Leisure Time

Most Iraqis work a six-day week that lasts from Saturday to Thursday. The only day of rest falls on Friday, which is the Muslim holy day. Iraqis spend most of their free time with family members and close friends. They go on outings or visit each other at home. After years of hardship, many people in Iraq have less money for leisure activities. They spend much more time at home.

Islam does not encourage men and women to mix with one another. Women only go out with female friends or family members.

During their long lunch breaks, some Iraqi men like to play backgammon.

In their free time, Iraqis like to watch films and television, read and listen to music. Chess and backgammon are popular board games. Iraqi men meet at cafes during lunch breaks and after work. There, they talk with friends and read newspapers. Women visit friends, while children play sports and take dance and music classes. Since the war, there are fewer celebrations and festivals.

Sports

Iraq's most popular game is football. Football is played in school playgrounds and parks across the country. Almost every neighbourhood has its own football team.

In Iraq, women also play sports. In the Muslim Women's Games, which are for female athletes from Islamic countries, women compete in events such as gymnastics and swimming.

Because sports are so popular in Iraq, the government often holds large competitions. This colourful display in Baghdad's national stadium marks the start of the Annual Police Games.

The Bedouin enjoy hunting with **falcons**, which are good at catching rabbits, **jerboas** and other animals. This Bedouin man wears a thick glove to protect his hand and arm from the bird's sharp claws, or talons.

Some Iraqis also enjoy sports such as basketball and volleyball. Popular individual sports include weightlifting and boxing. Many Iraqis like to attend sporting events in person but the larger events are broadcast on television, too.

Holidays

Iraq observes both official holidays and religious holidays. During the official holidays, all public offices, businesses and schools are closed. These holidays are New Year's Day (1 January), Army Day (6 January), Baghdad Liberation Day (8 February), Food and Agriculture Organization (FAO) Day (17 April), Labour Day (1 May), Republic Day (14 July), Peace Day (8 August) and Iraqi Independence Day (3 October).

Muslim women recite prayers during the Eid al-Fitr festival.

Before 2003, the Ba'ath Party held Revolution Anniversary Day parades.

Iraqi girls march in a street parade to mark the arrival of spring. In addition to such local festivals, Iraq hosts gatherings of artists, writers and poets from all over the world.

Religious Festivals

Eid al-Fitr (EED AHL-fitr) is a three-day festival at the end of the Muslim holy month of Ramadan. Eid al-Adha (EED AHL-ad-ha) is celebrated at the end of the *hajj* (HAAJ), or pilgrimage, to the holy city of Mecca, in Saudi Arabia. Iraqis also honour the prophet Muhammad's birthday. The Shi'ite holiday Ashura (as-SHOO-rah) remembers the religious **martyr** Imam Hussein.

Food

Iraqi cuisine is rich and varied. Their dishes do not contain pork or alcohol because Islam forbids these two items. Iraqis enjoy rice, yogurt, pitta bread and kebabs, which are chunks of meat grilled on sticks. One Iraqi specialty, *masgouf* (MAAS-goof), is made with fish. Other popular dishes are *quzi* (KOO-zee), or stuffed roasted lamb, and *kibba* (kih-BAH) which is fried meatballs.

Masgouf is a traditional Iraqi dish of grilled fish with sliced onions and tomatoes. The dish is often served with bread.

Lavish meals such as this one were more common before the Persian Gulf War. Since the war and the collapse of the economy, however, food has become scarce and very expensive in Iraq.

All meals are generally eaten with *samoons* (SAH-moons), or traditional bread. Iraqis also have a fondness for sweets. A very popular dessert specialty is *baklava* (baa-KLAH-vah), a pastry filled with honey and nuts. Additional desserts include *murabba amar* (moor-ah-bah AH-mar) and *zlabiya* (zlah-BEE-yah), with both dishes made from dates. To finish off the meal, Iraqis often drink Arabic coffee or sweet tea after dinner and eat fresh fruits.

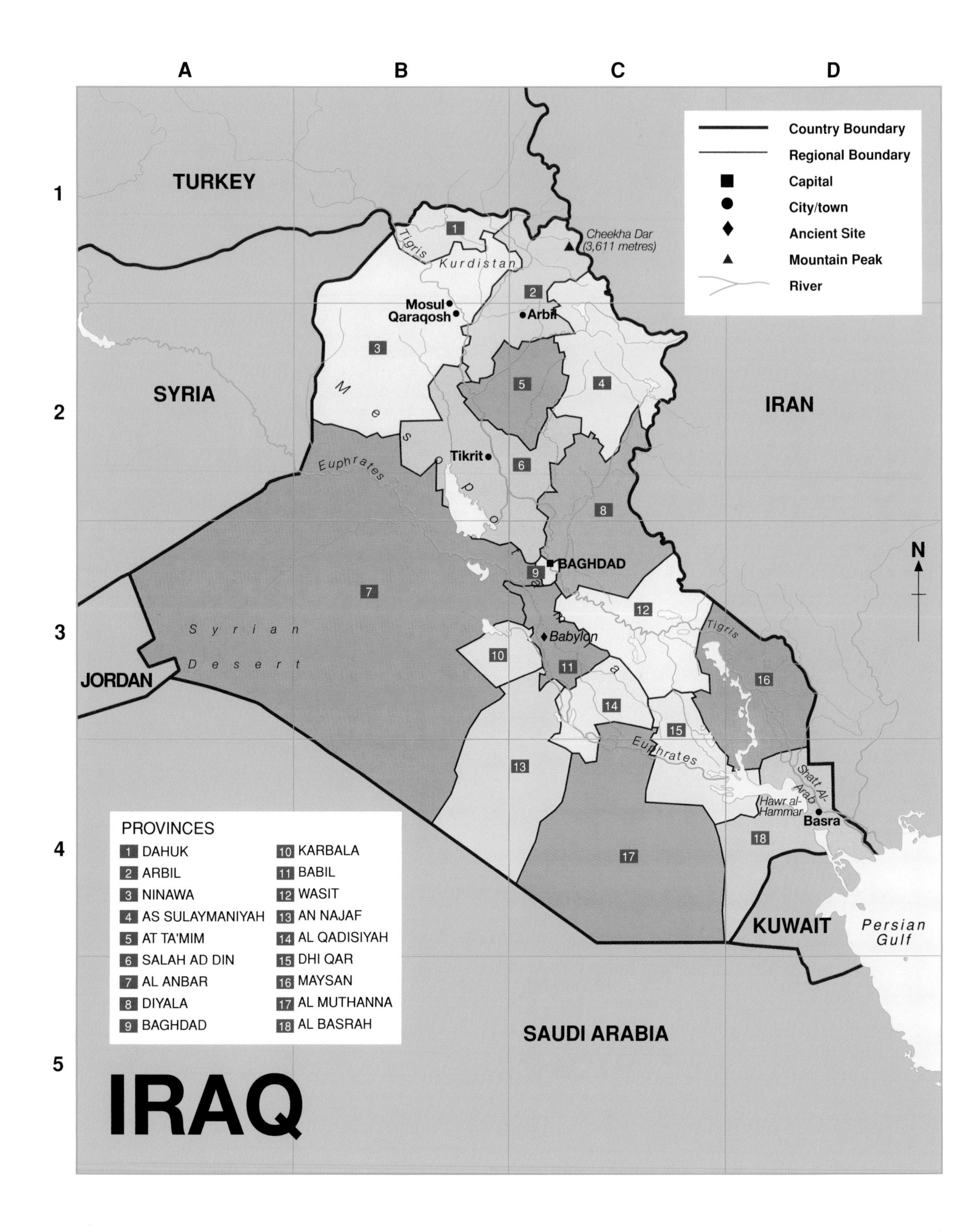
A
B
C
D
1
2
3
4
5
Country Boundary
Regional Boundary
Capital
City/town
Ancient Site
Mountain Peak
River
TURKEY
SYRIA
IRAN
JORDAN
KUWAIT
SAUDI ARABIA
Persian Gulf
Cheekha Dar (3,611 metres)
Tigris
Kurdistan
Mosul
Qaraqosh
Arbil
Mesopotamia
Euphrates
Tikrit
BAGHDAD
Syrian Desert
Babylon
Tigris
Euphrates
Shatt Al-Arab
Hawr al-Hammar
Basra
N
PROVINCES
1 DAHUK
2 ARBIL
3 NINAWA
4 AS SULAYMANIYAH
5 AT TA'MIM
6 SALAH AD DIN
7 AL ANBAR
8 DIYALA
9 BAGHDAD
10 KARBALA
11 BABIL
12 WASIT
13 AN NAJAF
14 AL QADISIYAH
15 DHI QAR
16 MAYSAN
17 AL MUTHANNA
18 AL BASRAH
IRAQ

The Ma'dan build their homes using reeds, which are found along the riverbanks.

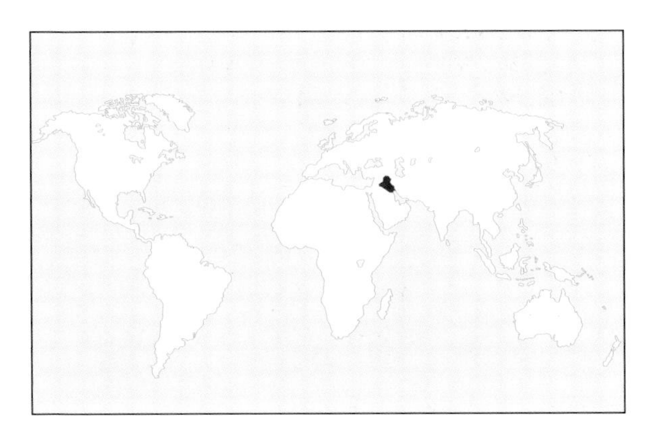

Quick Facts

Official Name Republic of Iraq

Capital Baghdad

Official Language Arabic

Population 28,945,657

Land Area 438,317 square kilometres

Provinces Al Anbar, Al Basrah, Al Muthanna, Al Qadisiyah, An Najaf, Arbil, As Sulaymaniyah, At Ta'mim, Babil, Baghdad, Dahuk, Dhi Qar, Diyala, Karbala, Maysan, Ninawa, Salah ad Din, Wasit

Highest Point Cheekha Dar, 3,611 metres

Major Rivers Euphrates, Tigris

Major Lake Hawr al-Hammar

Main Religion Islam

Major Holidays New Year's Day (1 January), Army Day (6 January), Baghdad Liberation Day (9 April), FAO Day (17 April), Labour Day (1 May), Republic Day (14 July), Peace Day (8 August), Iraqi Independence Day (3 October)

National Anthem 'Land of Two Rivers'

Currency Iraqi dinar (1,758 IQD = £1 in 2010)

Camels are one of the few animals that can survive in the heat of Iraq's deserts.

Glossary

arabesque: a style of art that uses the outlines of geometric shapes, fruits or flowers to make a pattern

calligraphy: handwriting done in a very artistic, graceful style

chant: to sing or utter sounds or words over and over again

conquer: to invade and take over a land using force

constitution: a set of laws that say how a country's government should be run and what rights citizens have

dictator: a ruler who has complete control over a country

empire: a very large collection of lands or regions ruled by one group

ethnic: related to a certain race or culture of people who have similar customs and languages

export: the process of selling and shipping products to other countries

falcon: a bird from the hawk family that people can train to hunt

inheritance: the act of receiving money, valuable objects or land after a family member has died

jerboa: a small, jumping rodent with long back legs and tail

liquorice: a plant that is often used to make sweets

martyr: a person who believes so strongly in a religion that he or she accepts death rather than give it up

monarchy: a system of government controlled by a king or a queen

mosque: a place of worship for Muslims

nomad: a person who moves from place to place, often living in tents

oppression: the cruel or unfair treatment of a group of people

phosphate: an acid that, when broken down, can be used to make bubbly drinks or be used in fertilizer

pilgrimage: a journey made to a holy place as an act of religious devotion

province: a region of a country with fixed borders and its own local government officials

republic: a country in which citizens elect their own lawmakers

technology: using machines to do jobs

uprising: an act of violence by citizens to fight against a government's rules

vocational: relating to a job, profession or skilled trade

workforce: people in a country who work, most often outside the home

For More Information

Books

Crean, Susan. *Iraq in Our World*. London: Franklin Watts, 2009

Islam, Hina. *An Eid for Everyone*. Bloomington, IN: AuthorHouse, 2009

King, John (Dr). *Kurds*. People under Threat series. London: Wayland, 2008

Laird, Elizabeth. *A Fistful of Pearls and Other Tales from Iraq*. London: Frances Lincoln Children's Books, 2008

Robinson, Anthony and Young, Annemarie. *Mohammed's Journey*. A Refugee Diary series. London: Frances Lincoln Children's Books, 2009

Senker, Cath. *Iraq*. Moving to Britain series. London: Franklin Watts, 2008

Wilkes, Sybella. *Out of Iraq*. London: Evans Brothers, 2009

Wiltshire, Katharine. *The Pocket Timeline of Ancient Mesopotamia*. London: British Museum Press, 2005

DVDs

About Baghdad. (AFD, 2005)

Iraq in Fragments. (Typecast Releasing, 2007)

My Country, My Country. (Zeitgeist Films, 2007)

Voices of Iraq. (Magnolia, 2006)

Websites

teacher.scholastic.com/scholasticnews/indepth/war-iraq/

Read an easy-to-understand overview of the war in Iraq and the steps being taken to rebuild the country.

www.infoplease.com/ipa/A0107644.html?pageno=1

Find out about Iraq's facts and figures, as well as an index that focuses on current affairs involving government, security and future stability.

www.timeforkids.com/TFK/specials/iraq/0,8805,424876,00.html

Keep up–to–date with the latest developments in Iraq.

Note to parents and teachers: Every effort has been made by the Publishers to ensure that these websites are suitable for children, that they are of the highest educational value, and that they contain no inappropriate or offensive material. However, because of the nature of the Internet, it is impossible to guarantee that the contents of these sites will not be altered. We strongly advise that Internet access is supervised by a responsible adult.

Index